Buried Music

BY THE SAME AUTHOR

Poetry
Overdrawn Account
Anaglyptya
This Other Life
More About the Weather
Entertaining Fates
Leaf-Viewing
Lost and Found
About Time Too
Selected Poems
Ghost Characters
There are Avenues
The Look of Goodbye
English Nettles
The Returning Sky
Like the Living End

Prose
Untitled Deeds
Spirits of the Stair: Selected Aphorisms
Foreigners, Drunks and Babies: Eleven Stories

Translations
The Great Friend and Other Translated Poems
Selected Poetry and Prose of Vittorio Sereni
The Greener Meadow: Selected Poems of Luciano Erba
Poems by Antonia Pozzi

Interviews
Talk about Poetry: Conversations on the Art

Criticism
In the Circumstances: About Poems and Poets
Poetry, Poets, Readers: Making Things Happen
Twentieth Century Poetry: Selves and Situations
Poetry & Translation: The Art of the Impossible

Peter Robinson

Buried Music

Shearsman Books

First published in the United Kingdom in 2015 by
Shearsman Books
50 Westons Hill Drive, Emersons Green
BRISTOL BS16 7DF

Shearsman Books Ltd Registered Office
30–31 St. James Place, Mangotsfield, Bristol BS16 9JB
(this address not for correspondence)

www.shearsman.com

ISBN 978-1-84861-389-8

Acknowledgements

Many of these poems or their earlier versions have appeared in *Agenda*, *The Battersea Review*, *Blackbox Manifold*, *The Cortland Review*, *English*, *Envoi*, *The Fortnightly Review*, *The London Magazine*, *The New Yorker*, *New Walk*, *Notre Dame Review*, *Poetry Salzburg Review*, *Poetry Wales*, *The Reader*, *Shearsman*, *Sitegeist*, *Stand*, *Tears in the Fence*, *The Times Literary Supplement*, *This Corner* and *The Warwick Review*. 'Like the Living End' was also anthologized in *The Captain's Tower: Seventy Poets Celebrate Bob Dylan at Seventy* (Seren, 2011). 'Another Dawning', 'For the Years', 'All Change', 'There Now', 'What Dawns' and 'Bohemian Interlude' were included in the *University of Reading Creative Arts Anthology* for 2012, 2013 and 2014. 'Rubbish Theory' appeared in *A Mutual Friend: Poems for Charles Dickens* (Two Rivers Press and the English Association, 2012). An earlier version of 'Volendam', the fourth section of 'Provident Scenes', appeared in the *Alhambra Poetry Calendar* (2013). 'Airgraphs' was published in *The Arts of Peace: An Anthology of Poetry* (Two Rivers Press and the English Association, 2014). Some of these poems were first collected in a chapbook, *Like the Living End*, published by Worple Press in 2013. My grateful thanks go to all the various editors and colleagues.

CONTENTS

ONE

TWO

In memory of
Thomas Fisher Robinson
1920-2011

One

Dirty World

'On n'écrit pas pour emmerder le monde'
        Raymond Queneau

Like characters in daytime comedy shows
glanced at through a mosquito screen
with its mesh unifying the scene,
our neighbours appear at French windows.

Against a scorching white wall, those people's
laundry droops on balconies.
Their block's new-planted sentinel trees
shrivel in noon stillness. Lombardy poplars

point towards cloudless, cerulean blue
above a shortcut to the shops.
Pallid grass, pallets and packaging collapse
like an overheated worldview

as its moral hazard, or lone mosquito voice,
hums past the speech-mark of our angle-poise.

For the Years

'…the remorseless passing
of the years.'
      Mark Ford

'You get through the years,' is what he said
beside night's un-let office space—
meaning mortgage payments to be made
or weather-threats up ahead.

But then they steal us from ourselves
and, no, I'm not myself today,
a memory of the living will, apology
for a past on bookshelves.

'You get through the years,' and what he meant
is debts would be paid—
us having a care, then, having our cares,
it being time we spent.

Another Dawning

starts a parody of indigestion
in the heat-pipes' creaks, ticks, knocks
as central heating switches on.
At last, the darkness cracks.
And now you know each return of the sun
is a miracle to insomniacs.

It's like we've been reprieved once more,
given this daily chance
to reach barely tangible rewards,
find some purpose or other
meaning as sunlight begins to gather
in blind slats at a window
thanks to the gift of a few words.

On the Edge of Illness

1. About the Sky

Beyond the pale of trees
and littered undergrowth,
there it is again, our moon;
full between bare branches,
it scuds near rooftop level
above a semi's chimney pots.
Full, or faintly on the wane,
seen suddenly, it takes a mind
off the day's absurdities …
Although we know about it now,
have been there, done that, still
intact it throws some light
on this road back home
disturbing dulled, automaton
limits with its milky glow
so un-bereft of mysteries
for no, not gone, they're there
at the edges of attention.

2. Duck Skaters

Dazzlingly cloudless day,
grassed spaces all a whiteness
as this ghosting ground-mist
mystifies the frosted lake,
duck skaters on their element
sense ice weaken, crack,
letting them take to it again
when they get the water back.

3. A Scored Day

Meanwhile, sun had gone on trying
as cloud-shapes made their way
across the slatted window panes
like melted music on a stave
past sheds, rust-eaten at their edges,
died-back plantings, other signs
of stubbornly rampant ivy hedges
crisscrossed by washing lines—
until a moon, egg-sliced by blinds,
rises in sky's deeper blue,
reminds you, smudged by further cloud,
of a broken night's sleep now;
and though there's no end of the world,
given all that's said or done
beyond your illness horizon,
it was as if nothing had happened.

In the Drift

Convalescent, by the Kennet side,
I see two raucous geese glide
down to a synchronized landing
through scattered waterfowl.
Cygnet nests built under wharves,
the pendant willows in a row
hold tints for the late spring's
promises of leaves
in branches' blurs, a greenish yellow.
A Fire and Rescue launch goes by
and, look, that ukiyo-e print
has a swan stood on the current
absorbed in waves of its headlong flow.

Feeling fragile, a memory of health,
it's my old self rehearsed
in piecemeal efforts at improvement,
finding unreal expectations
blight even what we do.
Stripped beds, the ring-fenced saplings
of a vanished factory's park
derive sense from resistless drift—
that incorrigible makeshift
devaluing, then revaluing things,
now the body politic
has to get its health back too.

All Change

Then next thing you know
from a partial leaf-fall
come re-emergent distances,
new chill factors, time
shifting more quickly, and loss is
sensed as that bit more precise
now raindrops lit by streetlamps
are speckling the panes
and thunderheads, a shorting day,
its crepitations over us,
again, they cover such a range
of start-lines at each terminus
making our last hopes first past the post,
as when a train manager cuts in to say:
'All change, please. All change.'

Rubbish Theory

'By which he probably meant that his mind would have been
shattered into pieces without this fiction of an occupation.'
    Charles Dickens, *Our Mutual Friend*

1

Now they're carting away the dust-heaps
on an earthmover and truck—
the pulverized halls impacted with work,
ink, tears and perspiration.
Hurrying through a quintessence of dust
blown into eyes and face,
we ghost past disturbance in the trees,
a flustered rustling at winter's end.
The dust-heaps catch what light there is
on a day rain-bearing wind
gusts remnant leaves about the place
and taking the register, ticking all boxes,
mind, I'll pay my way
with this fiction of an occupation …
Year on year,
I'll be guessing who those characters are
or dropping into poetry
despite each sudden blast, each blight;
now dust-heaps disappear.

2

The streets are paved with takeaway
wrappers, strewn sheets, cans
and posters for elections …
Attenuated traipsing figures
have their shadows stalking them,

each with a private memory
migrant to this point.
Sun sets on brick and greenery.
More distant figures come—
those struggling to get here,
others who'd not made it
and you that have, uncertain eyes
at checkout till or queue.

3

From blue-grey rain-fronts cut with sun
one slant, mitigating ray
back-lights the whole equivocal scene.
A bus runs through old factory
dockland this late afternoon—
its slums of possibility,
olfactory traces quite gone in thin air.
The dusk glows over familial faces
and matter out of place is
glinting with a change of weather,
mind or heart, if chance would have it
and, no, we'll never, never, never …
Love, we'll pay our way.

Coincidences

for Tim and Jo Dooley

Uncanny that we should be journeying home
in the one compartment underground,
but somewhere between King's Cross and Baker Street
over the Hammersmith & City Line's roar
I was sure that the words were 'poetry review'
and then a swallowed chuckle or a laugh,
your signature style, and it was you—
Orpheus on his route back from a reading …
Me too; and it was uncanny enough
in the vast metropolis, our subterranean coincidence;
uncanny, but apt we should meet this way
only a moment before you got off,
the train door sliding shut between us …
still more left to say.

Uncanny, but then again meeting that way
fitted well with your calling, this serious game.
Fellow travellers, underground,
and after inspiration, Eurydice, a loved one
or reaching toward new readers,
we'd waited for cadences slowly to form;
had conjured from nowhere the ghost interlocutors,
characters, their lives coinciding
a moment to gather discrete turns of phrase
for the traded confidences
snatched between Tube stations.
How they tune in above circumambient noise,
are lost from sight in your conurbation's
little streets hurled against the great—
its darkness, solitude, silences …

Reading in an Afterlife

Here I am reading in an afterlife
to eyes of family, friends, a mentor,
others I'd hoped to emulate
and conscious of what's passed on,
like by no means a Robinson
Crusoe, I've debts left too late
to repay: so whatever was meant or
published reads as if bereft.
But when I glance up they're attentive.
At last, beyond prizes or praise,
polite to a fault, they chiefly live
in such dreams of their posthumous days.

Next to Nothing

Through a watery light of after-rain
this bed, its personal history,
brought back by container ship from Japan
shows in ruffled covers
lines that say love spent the night here,
its indentations, your body's traces.

This commonplace bed with everyday sheets,
its rumples and creases
caused by the nightmare disturbances,
forms a tableau of shadowy folds
where by contrast time
tries to recover us, in all senses.

Yet still this unmade double bed
while you are away
preserves outlines where your body lay,
reminding me what lovers
do in their proximity
although I'm next to nothing now.

Between Parentheses

Most times, I'm like a multi-storey car park
where we can't find the car.
Overcrowded or deserted, in an oil-stained half-dark,
I go from floor to floor.

But today, through a long spring evening,
transparent shadow is equally spread
over this back-street brick and sandstone;
re-foliate flora cresting the hill,
that couple are training their spaniel
to 'Walk on!' 'Sit!' and 'Heel!'
as they each drop into a Polling Station.
Two lovers pause to kiss. Illuminated,
a gardener stoops among her flowers
when all a life's conflated
into that view of brief duration ...

It's as if I could see me now.

Note to Self

At a pavement edge, which separates
this moment from the next one
and the next, you see
yourself, that other person
on whom the mute phenomena
impose their lack of reason
or rhyme.
           You have the scented branches
of cherry, laburnum, magnolia
whose pale green growths revive.
Lifted, pointing in breeze they thrive
at blossom time while you,
alive in every minute,
might have a quiet word
for the solitude.
             You can't escape
that thought of being woken
in the small hours by those
cries of revellers strayed down your street,
inebriated woman's cries:
'I'll call the police and have you arrested;
you bastard, it's what you deserve',
their echoes.
             Still between skylines'
brightening you heard
birdsong like estate agent signs
and can't escape that thought,
as if the song birds sang
were *guess I'm doomed to be*
chained to a mem-or-y.

Airgraphs

'nel mezzo di una verità'
    Eugenio Montale

'Somewhere in Sicily', in 1943,
it went a long way
did army pay.

Under canvas in an almond grove,
there, you could solve
'your worst problem—washing',
as you wrote home to your mother.
'A local housewife is doing it for me,'
and her husband only charged 3 shilling.

You could get a new spring in your watch for 5,
which did seem 'very cheap'.
There were 'peaches, pears, lemons and grapes'
in Sicily, somewhere, that September '43.
Eggs were 'obtainable at 4d'
or 6 if you were foolish …
and reading your airgraphs, dad, what I see
is a steel helmet 'always full' of lemons.

Ein Feste Burg

'My hope to follow duly …'
    John Ernest Bode

1

Towards the parents' trysting places
as coxes call out stroke-rates
again I'm entertaining fates,
mine among them, reading traces
to call on others' memories
from these rock-bulwark circumstances.

Gut-strung rackets in their presses
still, when I was young—
they're courting on a tennis court
one far post-war summer,
the pair of them, divided,
constrained between its lines.

Now as the Wear brings me round
back to where we started from,
its geometry of space is
filled with my attempts to reach them
and arriving, a survivor,
well, I shall restore amends.

2

I'll wonder then what were the chances
they'd be falling for each other
by this gorge's riverside,
(mum come down the road from Shields,
dad home out of Palestine)

falling along wood paths just taken
under ramparts, ivied walls,
and wonder too what were the chances
his regatta crew would throw
their winning cox into the water,
caught by mum's Box Brownie camera:
so I can see him now,
see all that was to follow
duly hanging in mid-air …

Like the Living End

for David Mather 1954–2010

'Home is where one starts from …
… old stones that cannot be deciphered.'
    T. S. Eliot, *East Coker*

'I stole away and cried.'
    Bob Dylan

       1

After all the journeying
suddenly you see it: our river
with its reaches in their estuary light,
the sandbank outlines at low tide
and streams flowing forward to Seaforth.

After all, the journeying
that took you from yourself forever
forever returns you, though not quite,
home being never the same—
but come here for a funeral
you have it, don't you, that bereavement
in every departure, like its foretaste,
and each return a fostering
of distances, the sun-glare
now it glints on far refineries
as we've rounded Weston Point.

Above the bridge, an easyJet
plane descends to the renamed airport,
and in its higher sky's
releases, burdens being lifted

from you into the uneventful air
were shaming re-stirred memories
of girls, Dave, drunken parties,
those all-night games of Hearts
while cars on Mather Avenue
or police dogs barking in their kennels
brought them back, and you
can start again from there.

2

This one's in a minor key,
its black notes to be borne in mind,
the accidentals, obbligatos,
all those terms I learned by heart—
con brio, lento, da capo al fine,
rallentando in that street,
unadopted, past St Catherine's,
the cobblestones tumbling away
to raw earth and rubble.

Although you can't go any more,
are out of touch, I've come
back to a map of unvisitable places:
Darlington Street, for instance,
memorials which don't match the scene
were terraces' sandblasted
smuts become a pinkish red—
the post-Orwellian word-face
with piss-pot, blocked waste-pipe,
a flight of locks and pier,
its self-esteem in your capable hands …

That's where my music teacher's house was,
where I would play the pieces,

her black door like an omen;
scolded, told off for not practicing enough,
would repeat that performance week after week.
But this late morning, momentarily lost
and driven here by accident,
it was as if I'd been
trespassing yet again on my own past.

3

Then the bridge, the bridge was
like a major variation
taking us over a railway line
when summer itself had seemed to shudder;
dazzling with its last gasp,
it had knocked the stuffing out of
those loiterers behind a hearse
in unclouded sunshine.

Underneath the yew trees
acres of headstones were shining around us:
our eyes adjusted to that glare;
pasts were hovering in the shadows
down Cemetery Road, at Ince;
mourners caught up with each other,
and surely dad had brought me here
when on funeral duty once.

So that now in its chapel of rest,
and shaking myself, I was like
some astonished archeologist
who's just unearthed your grave-goods:
black vinyl discs, tapes, silver CDs,
headphones, and a new guitar,
East Coker's measured words—

distractions for an afterlife,
your music, your music wherever you are.

4

No, the dead can't live on bread alone
and, at it again, I'm co-opting them
for my own purposes
as when, assuming no way back,
home literally never the same,
we did revisit here once, remember?

Remember us wandering in that graveyard,
its separate plots grid-referenced
as on a street map, numbered
and spelt out along the low walls?
Then the present incumbent accosted us:
trespassing, we were trespassing
on his pastures, in a word.

But, told, he graciously showed us around
that past: subsided church porch
where under our feet coal-seams had collapsed,
and his vicarage lacking some upstairs rooms
for, saving costs, they had altered its roofline,
demolishing the one
in which my sister was born, later mine—
a space of thin air;
there, I heard him on Radio Caroline.

5

Then I'd have to get out of the house again,
traverse old love's domain
across Mather, this Friday morning,

then Menlove Avenue (another pun there)
to Quarry Street and Newstead Farm
built from warm sandstone cut out of its hill;
it brings home all our pining.

Treading down indecipherable stones
anew, like a revenant-returnee,
that vicar's son from *Cranford*,
I come back in the nick of time
to local librarians beginning their day
down shelves where love began
for you, Dave, making my drunken words
wrong as can be, after all our pining,
and sluggard children are taken to school
this September morning.

Though the past used to be another country
now a film truck's parked amid groves
by remnants of Allerton Towers
and, yes, our yesterdays, all of them,
turn into fiction, for grim
death would put an end to our loves.

6

The golf course in those grounds
of its tumble-down estate
has columns, plinths, an obelisk
in the local sandstone
seen taper into sky last spring;
yes, and like that time before
by way of convalescing,
I made a fairway tour.

Chestnut candles rose behind
laburnum tendrils, and
an aging intellect might turn
to the new wisteria,
but couldn't compete with them and their
natural recurrences—
surviving through broad daylight.

Uncanny in both senses,
life histories among neglect
at such dilapidations,
old stones that cannot be deciphered
have grown forgetful now,
as if those years had never happened ...
oh and the crumbling relations
here, at an eighteenth hole,
are fallen blocks, tagged stones;
like it's the living end.

7

Still I see myself leaping from the wrong train,
guitar-case in hand,
as it headed not for Durham
but on towards a siding
that weekend, the time we first heard
his 'Simple Twist of Fate'
when I came to visit in Providence Row
so that girlfriend of mine could meet her other
lover, though he didn't show ...

One of your mourners had quoted the album,
you making us 'lonesome when you go'
and Hawys, your distraught widow,
clutching at her photographs

for love's not most nearly itself under starlight
or lamplight with a family album
(forgive me, forgive me I'm co-opting *you* now).

But what else can I do with our dead ones
as we become people from history too?
Glad to be of use, you're helpful still,
don't want to cause her pain,
practising duets with me
like this one in a minor key
with black notes to be borne in mind?
Let's try it one more time again.

On the Esplanade

'And with Thy Spirit' upon the water
this late afternoon there's a sunlit mist
blurring outlines on that Wirral shore;
there's nothing afloat but the marker buoys,
apparently no one in Cressington Park.
I'm trespassing, like, on its front once more
as into a general amnesia go
all the babies he baptized,
the thousands married, churched and buried,
who prided himself on his good funerals ...
'Remember them, dad?'
                                        'Do I have to?' he said,
those words come murmuring back to me
now low tide laps at mud and rocks
and I'm alone along the last
stretches of Grassendale Esplanade,
stopped by the wartime pillbox
still guarding an entrance to Garston Docks.
Then, look, two blackbirds, male and mate,
come pecking at somebody's dusk patio
as if life were a table laid.

Diminishing Returns

'He is not here'
    Alfred Tennyson

Like he was dawdling still at the curb
outside his favourite restaurant
in Duke Street with its Chinese name,
I saw my father one last time.

The sign's attached to a derelict façade.
Weeds sprout from cracked guttering
or cling between the brickwork.
Buddleia phalanxes are picketing its door,

        *

its boarded-up door, back to our past,
and us warned not to enter ...
So let's not talk about sins of the father,
unless to forgive them in ourselves.

'That isn't him,' the rector said
(we were bidding farewell to his ashes),
'He has fallen asleep in the Lord.'
Lord, let us then depart in peace ...

        *

I'd seen the July hedgerows
haemorrhaging poppies
as the heavens opened—
a jack-knifed artic causing our delay.

Yes, we'd struggled north to find
the undertakers taking him
to Anfield Crematorium
with its cold-store morgue.

*

Making more unscheduled journeys,
again we passed the mannequins'
torsos, detached heads, limbs
hooked on a run-down warehouse wall.

Like conflicts playing out in us,
again the seagulls cried
and echoed about deserted streets
that Sunday, the week dad finally died.

*

Then back home from the Crem,
'He isn't here,' another said
in reply to an unheard question
(United Utilities cold-calling the dead).

But look, now pigeons flutter, see,
off into that dark recession
from their perch high on its ledges
guarded by glass shards.

Holy Dying

'you do not wholly die'
    Donald Justice

Sleeping in the parents' bedroom
where dad died
(now that mum's moved into the guest one)
no ghost tried
to bring word from an afterlife,
confess things done or left undone ...
Then to sleep
so soundly in the room where he had died,
to wake with no spectres in morning light
barely sensed through the curtain gap
as traffic on a rainy avenue
slid by outside,
meant clearly he was well and truly gone
to live in us—spectators
of shadows on repainted bedroom walls,
relatively rested in the dawn.

Two

There Now

Heavy and drooping, this year's new leaf
lifts in a breeze-filled dawn.
It oscillates, nods or dips as if
our life depended on
such a complete coincidence
of motive airs and sun.

As branches bend to whatever rhythm
isobars follow
forming expressions of interest with them
in the here and now,
you've to let him off, let him go and leave,
and allow yourself to grieve.

So chance would have it, making sense
at the edges of attention.
It says as much: his times are turning,
nothing's left for him here now
but traces of your failed mourning
in a new leaf on that bough.

The Late Returns

1. Another Twilight

Allow the point of the Coccodrillo,
its hazy cypress trees in profile
like a rough sketch for the Isle
of the Dead, as seen from yellow

stucco, his Villa Igea where Lawrence
finished *Sons and Lovers*, wild thyme
scenting olive-grove grass, crime
scenery come back to more than once.

Again you're mirrored in lake shadow,
a white sail flaking on its turquoise
wavelets, kept awake by traffic noise
along the Gardesana ... and you know

that this beauty's unbearable as before
even if seen from its opposite shore.

2. The Bird of this Place

As seen by the cormorant up on its rock
(or a remnant of coastal defences)
turning his head through one-eighty degrees,
sun-pilgrims gather on Palmaria's shore
with Portovenere house-fronts opposite;
unruffled old cormorant,
he's checking out the state of things
from his sentinel point on this late summer day.

Back to that turmoil of boats in the strait
—more than ever for him to ignore—
this emblem-bird might be studying the sky
or else looking down on the amateur swimmers,
two girls who splash about nearby.
Then he defecates suddenly into the water
to put off his taunters, those two laughing girls,
and won't budge, but holds his head high.

3. On a Title

'in piccola parte paesaggi robinsonici'
Antonio Tabucchi, *Racconti con figure*

In this cavernous, deserted bar
I'm dithering over a title or two
as Apennine hills at a distance
turn to silhouettes in sunset's glow.

That sunset's clouds are perfectly placed
to splay red rays across the plain;
they colour a parking-lot Stop sign
and one with Pedestrian walking too.

Perhaps because we've got to go
tomorrow and leave behind again
the so much more that's dear to you,
down shelves of matter for the plane

is this why I'm betting on the promise of a title?
In hope of what its words might do?

4. Cosmic Exile

Being given new directions
via a mobile phone
when we turned from the small piazza,
looking lost in space
between its gauntlet of façades,
there loomed a great disc, full, or on the wane.

Then with that mournful boom
of tyres over cobblestones,
and an orange ball
filling up its windscreen,
it was as if our red Ibiza
were heading for the moon.

5. Late One Afternoon

for Ornella

Grapes empurpling on vines,
the Japanese anemones
and fuchsias have grown tall;
small tendril leaves, splayed veins
of fronds turned by the breeze,
their shadows on a wall
move and set me thinking of
birds come down to pick at them,
a still-life cornucopia
and its occluded theme—
which could be 'ripeness is all'
in an apple tree you saw
uprooted, on a skip,
the red ones clinging to each bough!

Beside our fruited plum tree
you're burying bruised windfall
flesh in its mass grave,
have spaded over sullen earth
and give away, or offer free,
the unblemished now.

Childhood Memory

for Matilde

Comes your first among the many,
brightness, unmoved shadow
etching outlines of façades,
apartments where a gasworks was:
that's your first one, hereabouts,
pink frontages, you tell me,
warmed in stronger daylight
beside the place mum lived when young.

Then on beyond a railway line
we go towards her birthplace, greyer
times, regimes, the leaden years ...
But yours is stucco in clear sunshine,

and you'll be barely three-years-old,
bedazzled by that plaster.
Dad gone ahead already,
you've to join him with your little sister.
You hear the one word *bidet*
and, looking up, can't see their faces,
but picture it all from above and behind
as if *sub specie aeternitatis.*

Puberty

for Giulia

1

In the bathroom to scold you, I find
an odalisque, my daughter
blurred by humidity, a moist-blind
mirror, perfumed water.
Reading in the tub you seem
overnight older and, me, I'm dumb struck,
irritation gone into steam.

2

Which recalls for me your look,
you saying 'Dad, I'm not the Devil!'
only a day or two before.
It's true and, me, I'm lost for words,
intimidated, still,
by a woman, neither devil nor
your daddy's little girl.

A Middle-Age Scene

Like Lucas Cranach had painted the scene,
your naked medieval Eve,
old Adam in a hurry, two
shamed, humiliated people—
you catch them through the steam
of a tiny bathroom ...
and if I'm him, an aged parent,
then it's my bride, your mother, who
suddenly is in tears
about whatever time may want
(though not cast out of anywhere
as its misted mirror clears).

The Passersby

'naturally the public mind was demoralized'
    Walter Bagehot, *Lombard Street*

1. Grey Squirrel

A squirrel in Russell Square garden
advances across russet leaf-fall,
not at all shy
of us, passing by.

Pertinent glances identify
his way back through the hedge;
white flashes edge
a mousy tail.

While that glimpse of hotel frontage
brings out a hoarded lifetime,
there's overcast sky
in his beady eye.

Ear twitched at the light-change roar,
he catches up some of his store
and with arched spine
makes a beeline

through wind-turned leafage, yet more
traffic noise, lit dust, when as per
usual crowds swarm
past us, going home,

and we're gone from the square.

2. A Tramp-Barge

Plumes of smoke from the chimneystack
on a tramp-barge stream above
the path between two waterways
at Jericho; here, it's hunkered down
as if for winter or the hard times coming.
Moored, kitted out with a bike or two,
heaped firewood, pot plants, that barge huddles up
in its shawl of black tarpaulin.

There's something in you drawn to it
as scents of fry pan bacon come
wafting on the rain-fresh air.
How it takes its chances for survival!
Aloof, anonymous, autonomous—
or it seems so to the likes of us
taking a wrought-iron bridge across
this slow canal in autumn.

3. Under the Eye

Should front-of-house have lost the plot
and be corpsing on the spot,
well, behind those scenes
better actors learn their lines
in the spoked shadows from a gondola wheel.
Its years of oversight would reveal
how funds like surface water,
bird notes or the airwaves' chatter
are soaked away in daylight.
They can't help corpsing on the night
and, inimical, you imitate
our *faux amis'* own secret state

of mind, being caught on someone's phone,
documenting demoralization
at the Thames parapet, so
sold downriver by that bank-side flow.

4. Given Up

Stuck in traffic, the Mercedes taxi
still beside a bus stop
with some moments' poor reception
before an easeful, baroque music's
re-tuned on the radio,
that's when my softly spoken driver
was saying 'He's just given up'
about this man we see …

The oddly swollen belly
bursting through a too tight shirt
and the flies undone,
he's munching at a takeaway
in our blustery afternoon
of scurried clouds and sun …

But though we were soon moving on
towards the rail station
it's him who starts our conversation,
our seeing eye to eye
about just why he's given up,
given up to the passing day.

4. Die Neue Sachlichkeit

Left here, outside a fitting room,
I'm suddenly aware
the women swarming round me
are some in surplus camouflage,
some fetish underwear
and don't know where to put myself.
It's like there's no such thing as kitsch
or veterans' limbs or cabaret
of fashion and remark—
remark! Which gets me thinking how
my schoolboy stamp collection
had *entre deux guerres* issues,
the Marks blacked out like censoring
with yet more zeros overprinted
as their money went to Hell
taking peopled avenues,
un-peopled, dying, with them.
Still, those mutton-dressed-as-lambs'
made-up faces, cracked façades
would put a smudged smile on the fear
of age, decay, that decade's times
and they're like panicked symptoms.
I'm symptomatic too
when, come back, you allow
advice, agree it doesn't suit you;
but this was shopping now.

6. Public Space

Ochre tints splotch whitened ground.
An oak-tree sapling stands alone,
late leaves intact in a field of snow.

Look, an identity tag around
its slender bark,
branches and leaves are to grow
in memory of a girl—
her name engraved on the metal plaque.
Etched in frost, that robust
tree resists sub zero
winter bite and gale-force blast.

7. That Inclement March

we were following the plough's tractor tracks
in slushy ice where a salting of snow
here, as it fell, picked them out in white shadow
like dust on the broken *Large Glass*
or, for that matter, aerial photos
locating ancient metropolis foundations …

Melt-water icicles were hanging from the eaves.
I had already fallen in the snow,
was feeling bruised; with her weak-hearted breaths
my friend began to slow
past evergreen leaves; still, on we'd go,
and quick enough not to catch our deaths.

To the Point

for Ornella

At a tipping-point in summer
with tired, bedraggled leaves'
deeper greens above us,
unexpectedly, you led me
to this further point
of vantage.
                    Chimney pots
below in serried terraces
across a river valley
and, visible opposite, hills
catch the twilight glow beyond;
it's like a thermal imaging
camera could plainly see
leakage of human warmth
from their crevices.
                    Accused
of things you'd never think
to do, you carefully survey
people settled down to supper
and I am made more conscious of
dusk's softness.
                    Out along
a silent Upper Redlands Road,
day's suddenly extended
over turbid, riparian margins;
viewpoints open for you. Love,
you've paid the customs duty
on bringing us this far.

Three

The Island Suite

'the certainty of a real place,
the island as it can be'
    Edward Upward

1. Twyford Down

Ground-mist rolled off downland
fills a southbound carriageway;
back-storied by cloud cover,
it muddles earth and sky.

A streaked dawn's cutting through them.
Cars rush for the coast—
confusions of cloud- and landscape
deepening as we come close.

Like variations on a theme,
each enigmatic shape
conceals that much you know you know
we have to miss today.

2. Cowes

More mist's flowing from the hills
onto a marina inlet;
it hazes over moored mast-work,
dockyards, sheds, yacht hulls …

Our ferry, slowing, penetrates it,
wrapped up in a past
of seaside artists' etchings—
as if what's lost weren't lost.

3. Brook Chine

At an ozone limit, breakers
on the littoral return
—us too, in silhouette, with others
together and alone.

The white gull-flocks in shallows
are paddling or paused
on seaweed-daubed red rocks.
Sauntering, our shadows

crisscross pebbles on the beach.
People stroll around its bay
past part-crumbled cliffs, the tide pools'
iterations of a cloud-heaped day.

4. Brighstone Bay

You notice run-offs from each chine
make umber, burnt sienna,
and yellow ochre paint-drips
about the day's duration.

Somehow, disparate forms of stone
by chance or intervention
appear as found, primeval sculpture
shown along the shore.

That's how your slowed attention
finds manifestos on this coast
for a style that will not veil,
no, nor teasingly reveal.

5. Compton Bay

Heads emerge from troughs
or are buffeted by waves.
Above, in stiffened breeze,
a seagull, stock-still, cries.

It accompanies our striving.
Still, the sea relieves
even that insignificance,
outliving us, surviving.

6. Newtown

Nothing less in this silted harbour
detains me round midday
but clinker-boats tied up to stillness
and an anchor on its chain.

Out beyond the salt-marsh wattles,
dilapidated seawalls,
time's and tides' withdrawals
maroon a mildewed slipway.

Ghosts of local populations
recalled for us from air
are half-reflected on low water,
their memorials in disrepair,

while the mirrored sky, a Dutch one,
is filled with sails, white swollen clouds
from ages back, the petals fallen
onto this nowhere, never, ever again.

7. The Needles

Something of that, now a fierce wind
batters Old Battery's emplacements,
and like a compass needle
is spinning us around.

It points to Palmerston's defences,
protection for our island story.
In the channel, between his Follies,
a coaster beats its way

at risk of shipwreck, which did happen
after that three-master lay
at anchor, as their brother wrote,
'beside the shores of Wight',

and happened later, photographed,
under lighthouse rock
when reminiscent mist closed in
blotting out its outline.

8. Farringford

Through bosky light, forgiven for
our accidental trespassing
out of an only curious
urge to see her laureate's house,

now, beside a golf course,
we see the disrepair
from its hotel incarnation …
But they were planning to restore

the poet's still kept silent workroom,
bring his desk back home,
and have the plantings as they were
on downland off towards that shore.

9. Brading Villa

'e poi torna alla luce con i suoi canti'
      Giuseppe Ungaretti

Everything else, as you'd expect,
comes into focus gazing down
towards a grassy haven—
an inlet once, where tribes would trade,

now over-built with bungalows,
though, whichever way you turn,
the buried port is excavated
like a found occasion.

10. Shanklin

Sun had mocked us through its shadows
all along the beach-hut suburbs
and retirement's accommodation
with families calling it a day.

But these resort towns still defeat me,
reddened skin surprised by sun
despite a coastal sky's
gleams given back off ocean.

We're steering clear of every groyne,
which council signs advise,
spouts fountaining through flagstone holes,
the breakers keeping time.

11. Bonchurch Shore

'Slow, like everything else here,'
that off-duty chef had said—
between two worlds, one dead,
the other powerless to be born,

I thought along East Esplanade
out towards Bonchurch shore,
water colourists' memories
tinting the spray back to Ventnor.

12. Sandown

Breeze quickened on its promenade
down the beach at sunset.
Undeterred, survivors
loitered on round town.

Offshore, still, container ships
were parked across the bay.
Closed emporia, charity shops
clung on in their way.

Then for last gasps of a Sunday
our innumerable childhoods
would haunt arcade and formica café
to fight off solitudes—

relieved most by a sparrow perched
on that painted terrace chair.
Meanwhile, sun-dazzle off the sea
casts askance rays over us,

and already whole lives later, waves
return below its pier
to bring back what's behind the times,
what could not disappear.

13. St Catharines

Imagine a lighthouse of your own:
it's how I would get used to these
squalls, amusements, pleasure domes'
ingrained dilapidation;

and, yes, I must get used to them,
ever more needful of assurance
to scare away dysfunctional
behaviour in this life.

Then there it was, St Catherine's Point,
towers, foghorns come in sight—
sold off now, a private house,
holiday lets in pristine white …

Look, though, its revolving beam
still darts past wind-bent trees
and on across surrounding blackness,
over those darker seas.

14. At Ryde

The lights of Southsea at a distance
beyond its Spithead Forts
decorate wide Solent waters
as when, sixteen, I'd not cross over

and spent the night right here
squatting on my rucksack
till the next day's early ferry
in crowds stuck at Ryde Pier.

Oh there are scenes you can't relive,
however willed, like idle tears
brushed from a chancellor's eyes
when pomp and all the circumstances

mourned those squandered years;
for even if it's not your death,
don't ask, but let that tanker hurry
back to its berth like a debt.

15. Solent Water

'die Kompaßnadel steht auf Nacht'
Ingeborg Bachmann

The compass needle turns to night,
night water, crossing the bar,
ship shapes in our vicinity
lit up like Christmas trees.

But now you see them, face to face
with that dark liquid, out on deck,
like an end to island stories
in the waves' embrace.

Four

What Dawns

'La notte lava la mente'
    Mario Luzi

Night can rinse the mind
whatever I might say
like rain in spattered waves
dissolving thought-tangles
through the dark hours ...
and Japanese anemones
opened towards dawn,
violet petals on their stalks
bow faintly in pinked air
waiting for some sun—
which comes along the rooflines,
blood-suffused, another day.

All Times are Local

for Giulia

1

Undaunting, your thousand-piece jigsaw
shows a projection of the whole wide world
and, done, it lies still on that table
like a reconstruction,
a reconstruction of our moments
separated by left times and spaces
put together here.

2

Although not far from Greenwich now
or Brunel's brick-arched bridge,
this gazing through your bedroom window
brings them back to mind—
the dusks on near or gone horizons,
and his first Great Western
instituting railway-time.

3

So it's about your own time too
and family resemblances
shifted by walls of chronometer dials,
each one dependent on further place-names
through transit lounge to boarding gate;
you've reassembled all of that
imagining returns to Sendai,
your nostalgia for Japan.

4

Love moves the attentive hand, the eye,
to recollect arranging shadows
long before railway- or clock-time;
it interlocks pieces, shows
through gleams from a scented candle flame
everything everywhere equally here
in world present tenses.

Themes on a Variation

'...in the best of all possible worlds.'
    Gottfried Leibnitz

1

Cloud forms fight it out with sun
while, walking home, we happen on
a woman, under willow fronds—
with yellow buddings down each bough;
she pauses, winded, at the bridge,
hand clutching its black balustrade;
then storm-light through those tendrils
flares above a multi-storey
in the one, only possible world

2

where that corner of a built-up island
has the scrawled graffito, saying:
'This is a photo opportunity',
a conflux, at which waters meet,
town structures crazed across its flow;
then here, the currents mingling
as if from a non-existent point
of view, in ripples before your eyes,
is the one world of all possibilities.

From Amsterdam

for Matilde

When, in point of fact,
as she left me to wander
round Ooster-dok and stand or
turn down Nieuwe Herengracht,

I was taken by gulls' cries
in search of our originals—
façades redoubled in its canals
cross-cut with cloudy skies.

                    *

Recalled by a clatter of trams
to be, like, shaking off
nostalgia for a life
unlived, past art- and ship-museums,

I drifted about as if to find
you or maybe youth again
on a stroll through the Waterlooplein,
its flea-market's time out of mind.

                    *

Careless hankerings would walk
those days back into place;
but, no, not a trace
of us across Vondelpark …

There, the drinkers on benches
blur grey, daylight hours
and time, no longer ours,
brings in its revenges.

*

Although strayed eyes alighted
on maritime sky above
but missed my youthful love,
simplified, slighted,

the gleam of unseen sea beyond
in reflections off its waves
sharpened architraves,
rooflines, a gable-end ...

*

Because world's brute opacity
looks that bit clearer cut
in such an even light, what
swells through this inquiring city

is the urge to understand
figured in Dutch architecture—
as if with words I could be sure
or poems, ô Spinoza, and

*

when lift-bridge lamps come on,
at twilight, seeing as I am
in 'unfathomable Amsterdam'
where a still wintry sun

had brought out all the colours—
really many more
than only three or four,
it calls up outcomes far from ours

        *

in glimpses of that Jewish girl's
smile caught by a camera
while bride and family appear
(her pilgrims queue now down canals)

and tells how relentless life recurs
with thoughts of a daughter
biking past swirled water
as she gets on with hers.

Provincialeweg

'I do not attribute to nature either beauty
or deformity, order or confusion.'
     Baruch Spinoza, *Correspondence*

Whatever lies beyond the lines
or today's noisy earth-mover
I'm lost trying to discover—

now as the Number 9 tram
advances before us, its sign
seen through an August thunderstorm,

                    *

as everything is wet with rain
out across Diemen's one third land
and two of cloud-strewn sky;

then there come silver birch trees
lining sun-flecked water,
leaves whitening in a haze.

                    *

Sheep shelter from high summer heat;
they've snuggled down by sea-waves
under breeze-turned foliage

and I can see you're scared for this one
away from its flock, in direct sun,
breathing fast and swollen.

                    *

But when a full moon rises
behind the waterside opposite,
sun's reflected as a finer light

on those stragglers left unknowing
what it might be if not this
flurry about the body's senses—

*

maybe tremors from the fronds
of ash before another storm,
in reed beds, Japanese knotweed,

seeding nettles, slug plagues
(whatever goes on beyond us
and keeps going …).

Provident Scenes

1. Amsterdam

Those coots have built their reed-nest here
on what must be a wooden floor tile
floating like some shipwreck's raft
down the middle of a sun-struck, still canal.

Hot, and in full flood we drift
slowly, slowly going past
yet more birdlife habitat—
a tarred, feathered corner of Watergrafsmeer.

That male strives back to where, alone,
he's left both rafting mate and chick,
a morsel firmly in his beak
for their not-yet-fully-fledged one.

2. Den Haag

A moribund crab's cracked by a seagull
on the beach at Scheveningen.
Bungee-jumpers plunge from its pier
swinging wildly in mid-air.

Coastal gusts have thinned the sea-line.
Its vast hotel's concealed from sight.
Precarious, then overwhelmed,
sand-walls collapse in a rising tide;

and yet what with the seagulls' cries
above our long symposia,
nowhere, love, can world be within us
without this one outside.

3. Otterlo

More confident, biking off ahead,
how your young back takes me back
to Gris, Léger, and Mondrian
still here to see despite the years ...

and after what was said, returning,
look, a double-dip recession
from this forest cycle track,
its barely undulating drop

through a dune-like landscape
of scrub-pine and the furze,
is unfolding all before us
gone back to go on.

4. Volendam

But chances I could un-encumber
something of my past aren't good
where we stopped to taste a roll-mop
one morning, that September.

As moving on the Ijsselmeer
are flotillas of white sails,
while birds' feet shadows lead the way
over café awnings

and couples on its harbour mole
may well be the likes of us,
black-headed gulls inviting me
to see lives as they are, and whole.

Van Gogh's *Jewish Bride*

'because she was fair to look upon'
    Genesis 26, 7

Think of the eyes, their middle-distance gaze,
the hands which tactfully touch;
think of a momentary stillness that says
they'll be together for ever,
un-movingly moving, and with such
tenderness between each lover.

Then think of his eyes, the living hand
that signed it *Rembrandt f*
thinking of their silent joy—
which might be his Titus and daughter-in-law's,
a sister by her brother
or, no, a husband sporting with his wife.

Then think of the one who can't tear himself away,
stands rooted in this place
and, directionless still, was heard to say
he would give ten years of life
for a fortnight at the Rijksmuseum
with that history-ed double portrait, face to face.

Bench Marks

for Roy Fisher

If you give me a piece of your mind
—one looking or formed like
a school desk fissured with inscriptions,
milk stains, that cracked varnish,
nooks, crannies, hearts, tokens,
marks of weakness, others' sorrow
where, synapses built from attention
wandered to drops as they blink in a rain-pool,
drenched leaf-mulch choking a gutter
or ripples on some surface water,
thought concentrates until you find
it and the world align.

If you give me a piece of your mind,
I'll use it for the peace of mine.

Bohemian Interlude

Bridal pairs snapped on Charles Bridge
jostle with the headless torsos,
more sorry body images
like symptoms in its art museums.

A balloon hangs above the Moldava.
Goya's *'sueño de la razón'*,
his *Desastres de la Guerra*
are never ever far away

       *

from Oska Kokoschka's balcony,
and those calligraphic vistas
which left such a mark on me,
as did his cartoon Munich breakfast;

likewise, the tidied up darkness
of a Franz Kafka display
foreboding fearful crematories
in the mind of Joseph K.

       *

Couples tread down autumn leaves
on an island in its river;
they haunt the Soviet-era benches,
watch barges nudging by—

as though trying not to discover
they're exemplary, like that family,
that one bit of socialist realism
allowed, still, in the gallery.

*

Come darkness, red-lit cellar bars
are possessed by hosts and others
debating what those years
might have meant, their wars'

horrors not lost, nor long ago;
then, locked in, after-hours
drinkers at least half reveal
their guiltinesses, sorrow …

*

Ah but with the dawn tomorrow,
light leans at a kitchen table;
from this foreign window
a hidden, weed-choked garden

stands in for all the distant vistas
onto exile's residues—
what will have been prompt reasons
to evacuate those views.

*

They're banished with the daylight
by a villa's parkland grotto,
Prague's hills gestured at below,
his castle, that balloon in flight,

the sad, odd, dangerous to know
nowhere to be seen now;
they go about their daily business,
and we've to let them go.

The Dandelions

Good for your eyes, the dandelions,
their hundreds and thousands, are suns
mistaken for a field of rape.

But, close up, every beam-like petal,
us striking out across a meadow,
has you flooded with its ray;

and in that haze of forget-me-not blue
among this Danaë shower, or crop,
did someone sow the ground with teeth?

Then down we went through dazzling yellow
where, love, tired, struck by them,
look, hovering insects live their day—

a good one, it had turned out, to have.

Inland Seagulls

Then their cries, redoubled at dawn,
recall for me a single seagull
drunkenly veering across
flagstones on Addington Road.
White wings outstretched to get airborne,
it was lunging down for food scraps
outside the crescent shops.
I thought: like Baudelaire's albatross
those giant wings impede its walking
or, injured, it can't fly …
But, no, up it flew above slate housetops
as if, that quandary outsoared,
now it could make back towards its seaboard
breeding grounds and sky.

Buried Music

Buried music from a life
(like quoting Rilke at the Co-op)
comes out with paddlers in the shallows,
their reflections reminiscent
of a Philip Wilson Steer—
while the rib boats, harbouring,
silhouettes in last light air,
are being dragged back up their slipway;
it accepts those local stones
in a graveyard near the long-stay
car park, here, a seaside
town where I could catch its tones
attuned to all the shingle pebbles
moved by a turning tide.

When the Leaves Drift

after Rilke

Look, now, a thick orange brushstroke
of light bisects the lake.
That full moon in a deep-blue sky
dots its *i* as I cross the park
to make it back from work alone.
Passing me, a woman's face is
up-lit by her mobile phone
while, about us, leaf-strewn traces
of this sublunary, lunatic life
and mad world, my masters,
turn a wearied head towards home.
In autumn, glad to have one,
I won't be answering more mail, love,
nor appear at our door downcast as
the way's caught by that bravura brushstroke
from a moon above.

Like a Railway Station

somewhere, on the edge of landscape
abstracted by deep autumn mist,
a grey-ness in the troubled woods'
threatened ash and remnant elm
as from a local train or platform,
its blur's this slow reminder—
'depending on your nearness,
forgive me, to the grave,' he says.

But I have had that thought already
with the various aches and pains;
and carrying my own inside me,
look out across deserted tracks
past people waiting on connections
to where fields fade in distance.
A voice announces some delays
and the distance takes no notice,

not having that much time for time.

Estrangement

Suddenly, winter trees
appear like ruined monasteries
and, further, through wrecked architraves,
under blown clouds' blanket cover,
grey skies, thinking, as you do,
why I see much clearer now,
again the season's distances
have shaken up our lives.

Then as circumstance would have it
in planning-blighted town or city
I find us living and lumping it, see,
with what creature warmth and comfort
we wrap about us for a start
in the distance's vicinity.

Grisaille

'We must not expend all our limited resources
trying to make water flow uphill.'

Come to think of it, the sky,
our big estuary sky
between one Christmas and New Year:
cloud cover all an off-whiteness,
blown plumes billow from far cooling towers;
now the bridge rises before us,
we're lifted above wide expanses of space;
and, look, terrace housetops,
chimneys, the water
separating Runcorn from Widnes,
and sandbanks exposed at low tide today
spread in an endless, a various
sublimity of grey.

Similarly high, come to think of it again,
here we are, suspended in glass,
crossing the solicitor's office space when
gone to sign those documents …
A riverfront greyness below,
we'd carried our untidy lives
from blustery street level, cluttering their atrium,
to a sight of cargo vessels
moored along the Wirral shore,
its ferry boats plying back and forth as before.

Everywhere recalled, come to think of it again,
there's always someone reminiscent
of a Rembrandt in old age—
behind his head, more clouded
skylines, flamed refineries,

and that house across the water,
its glints of windows in a dusk
looking back at us, as are his patient eyes.

Then the flow of money, come to think of it again,
with immigrants and emigrants
swarming on those waters,
I can sense them as we sign,
are tied in legal ribbon
here with memorials of this city
(ship models in their cases)
aground on its ebb tide.
Then we manage our descent to the grey outside.

Absurdly useful, come to think of it again,
poetry down these avenues
drawn from valve murmurs in the poor trees,
their wind-twitched branches, stirred
rhythms of a labouring heart,
is offering its words,
its advice about how to survive—
given what's occurred,
with Liverpool stretched out below your ward
and beeping life supports I heard.

But leaving you, mum, come to think of it again,
still I glimpse the seagulls'
flocks of white flecks feeding
over exposed sandbanks,
can see the dripping trees
with calligraphic bark, boles, branches
and some water flow uphill
at extremes of windscreen wipers,
us driven off towards
the bridge down this same city's boulevards.

Expanse Hotel

'C'est la mer allée
Avec le soleil.'
    Arthur Rimbaud

Staring again at our northern sea
from my fourth-floor window,
I'm dazzled here as high tide waves
bear in on its cube of light,
recalling background sounds surf made
pointed to by worn green groynes,
their exhalations all last night
like a loved one's snoring …
Stiff breezes down the promenade,
they gave you back yourself
late in the day, late as might be,
what with the faint spray on your face …

Then looking from this hotel room
on the front at Bridlington,
I ask you, could a glimpse of these
cars reversing in to park
have brought back living memories
of far scenes blanked by chores, cares, years?
Or could, when all is said,
the sight of a sea-line's isolate expanses
solid in this solar brightness
with cliff paths, crumbling, coax our shadows
round the curve of Bridlington Bay
as far as Flanborough Head?

Notes

Dirty World: The epigraph ('One doesn't write to dirty the world') is a remark Raymond Queneau made in a 1953 interview.

For the Years: The epigraph is from Mark Ford, 'White Nights', *Seven Children* (London: Faber & Faber, 2011), p. 22. His spoken words inspired the poem.

Rubbish Theory: The title is from Michael Thompson's 1979 volume of the same name. The epigraph is from Charles Dickens, *Our Mutual Friend* (1865) chapter 8, in which Mr. Boffin encounters lawyer Lightwood's clerk Blight. The allusion to 'Rule Britannia' at the poem's end, and other brief phrases, also appear in this episode or elsewhere in the novel.

Note to Self: The song cited at the end is 'Chained to a Memory' (1964) by Betty Everett.

Airgraphs: The epigraph, meaning 'in the midst of a truth', is from 'I limoni' [The Lemons], the first poem in *Ossi di seppia* (1925).

Ein Feste Burg: The title is from Martin Luther's c. 1529 hymn, 'a strong fortress', the epigraph a phrase from 'O Jesus, I have promised' composed in 1868. My mother's Christian name is Julie.

Like the Living End: The epigraph from 'East Coker', the second of *Four Quartets*, cites phrases from the final passage in the poem, read as part of David Mather's funeral service at Wigan Crematorium, Ince, on 2 September 2010. Bob Dylan's 'He was a Friend of Mine' was played in tribute to his lifelong obsession with the singer's work, an obsession I share.

Diminishing Returns: The third verse of *In Memoriam* part 7 begins: 'He is not here; but far away / The noise of life begins again'.

Holy Dying: The poem's title is borrowed from Jeremy Taylor, *The Rule and Exercises of Holy Dying* (1651). Its epigraph is the final phrase in Donald Justice's 'Sonnet to my Father', *Collected Poems* (New York: Alfred Knopf, 2005), p. 23.

Another Twilight: The Coccodrillo [Crocodile] is on the Verona side of Lake Garda. The Villa Igea is in Gargnagno, while the Gardesana is the road running along the Brescia side of the lake through Salò and other places associated with the 1943-45 puppet Republic.

The Bird of this Place: Palmaria and Portovenere are at the entrance to the Bay of Lerici.

On a Title: The epigraph is from 'Ritratti di Stevenson', one of the stories in *Racconti con figure* (Palermo: Sellerio, 2011), p. 225.

Late One Afternoon: 'Ripeness is all' is a phrase of Edgar's in *King Lear* (act 5, scene 2, line 11).

A Middle-Age Scene: Lucas Cranach the Elder painted a number of images of Adam and Eve, including a 1526 painting now in the Courtauld Institute, London.

Die Neue Sachlichkeit: The title, meaning 'The New Realism', was used to designate a group of painters in Weimar Germany, including Georg Grosz and Otto Dix.

The Island Suite: The epigraph is from 'The Island' in *The Railway Accident and Other Stories* (Harmondsworth: Penguin Books, 1969), p. 230. The epigraph ['The compass needle stands on night'] to 'Solent Water' is from 'Totes Hafen' [Dead Harbour] in *Die Anruf des Grosse Bären* (1957); that to 'Brading' ['and then returns to the light with his songs'] is from 'Il porto sepolto' [The buried port] in *L'allegria* (1919).

What Dawns: The epigraph is from 'La notte lava la mente' [Night washes the mind] in *Onore del vero* (1957).

Themes on a Variation: The epigraph's famous assertion was first published in French in *Essais de Théodicée sur la bonté de Dieu, la liberté de l'homme et l'origine du mal* (1710).

From Amsterdam: 'ô Spinoza' is from Max Jacob's 'Poème dans un gout qui n'est pas le mien' in *Le Cornet à dés* (1945); 'unfathomable Amsterdam' is the translation of Vittorio Sereni's phrase 'insondabile Amsterdam' from 'Dall'Olanda', *The Selected Poetry and Prose of Vittorio Sereni* trans. Peter Robinson and Marcus Perryman (Chicago: University of Chicago Press, 2006), p. 183.

Provincialeweg is a road in the southeastern outskirts of Amsterdam. The epigraph is from Letter XV to Oldenburgh (1675).

Van Gogh's Jewish Bride: Rembrandt's *The Jewish Bride* hangs in the Rijksmuseum, Amsterdam. Vincent Van Gogh said of his autumn 1885 visit that 'I would give ten years of my life if I could sit here before this picture a fortnight with nothing but a crust of dry bread for food.'

Bench Marks: This poem is a response to Roy Fisher's 'Bench'.

Bohemian Interlude: An exhibition of Goya's etchings was on show in Prague when I visited with Tom Phillips in October 2012. Oskar Kokoschka lived there from 1934-38. *The Red Egg (*1940-1), a satire on the Munich Agreement, hangs in Prague's Modern Art Gallery.

Inland Seagulls: The seagull's movements were reminiscent of those described for his bird in Charles Baudelaire's 'L'Albatros' from *Les Fleurs du Mal* (1857).

When the Leaves Drift: My poem is remembering 'Herbsttag' from *Das Buch der Bilder* (1902). Here is my previously unpublished version of the poem, called 'Autumn Day':

> Lord: it's time. The summer was so vast.
> Cast your shadows over the sundials,
> and over fields let wind gusts pass.
>
> Command the last fruits to ripen fine;
> give them two more south-like days,
> push them to completion and convey
> the last sweet notes to bodied wine.
>
> Whoever has no house now, won't build one.
> Whoever's alone now, will remain so later,
> will watch, read, write long letters
> and anxiously drift up and down
> the avenues, when the leaves scatter.

Grisaille: The epigraph is a remark made by the then Chancellor of the Exchequer Sir Geoffrey Howe in 1981. It was first made public just over thirty years later on 29 December 2011.

Expanse Hotel: The epigraph, 'it's the sea gone / with the sun', is from 'L'Eternité' (May 1872).

www.ingramcontent.com/pod-product-compliance
Lightning Source LLC
Chambersburg PA
CBHW020213090426
42734CB00008B/1044